W9-ATN-447

Slide and Slurp, Scratch and Burp

More about Verbs

To Isabella
—B.P.C.

Slide and Slurp, Scratch and Burp

More about Verbs

by Brian P. Cleary

illustrated by Brian Gable

M MILLBROOK PRESS / MINNEAPOLIS

Verbs are words like sneak and sniff,

sneeze and seize

and wheeze and whiff.

Planting carrots,
getting traction,

Verbs give sentences
their action.

You might be exploring the Alps or the Amazon, maybe restoring the chair that your grandma's on.

or hitting
or roping or biting—

Verbs can make sentences
very exciting.

They tell us of horses

that nuzzle and nip,

of bears as they guzzle

and birds as they sip.

8

They tell us of scooters both **swerving** and **stopping,**

throws that are curving or sliding or dropping.

So wrap a package, tie a knot,
clap your hands, or cry a lot.

Triumph, tremble,

trot, and trample,

you'll use a **verb**
for each example!

Fly to the flower shop,
dash to the dance,

swing by the swimming pool,
frolic in France.

Soar to the circus and float to the fair.

Without verbs, your sentence can't go anywhere.

Each sentence **has** a subject—
it's kind of like the star.

It's what the whole thing's all about:

Dave's dish,

Mom's look,

Todd's car.

Subjects always need a Verb—
it's what makes fishes swim

and lanterns light
and writers write
and clippers cut and trim.

Some Verbs aren't the action kind—
They "link" instead of "do,"

connecting sentence parts, as in,
"Your dog appears quite blue."

These linking verbs
connect a subject
to a word or phrase

that's called a
Subject complement.
It's done in lots of ways:

It became ridiculous.

That strudel sure smells great.

The crime remains a mystery.

This play seems second rate.

The forms of "be"
are linking verbs,

like, "Are your names Michelle?"

Were and was
work this way, too—
they're forms of "be" as well.

I am Shannon.
He **is** Mort.

Were you the one
who **was** in court?

There **are** times
a form of "be"
is all that's **needed**, Verbally.

Whether you slide

or you slip

or you slurp,

if you should scream

or you scratch

or you burp,

if you're making a fraction
or writing a blurb,

because there is action,
you know it's a verb.

So if you should gloat

or you glisten

or listen,

say to the chef,
"Take that out and put this in,"

Whether you pounce

or pronounce

or perturb,

I'm here to announce
that you're using a verb!

So, what is a verb?

Do you know?

ABOUT THE AUTHOR & ILLUSTRATOR

BRIAN P. CLEARY is the author of the Words Are CATegorical©, Math Is CATegorical©, Adventures in Memory™, and Sounds Like Reading™ series. He has also written The Laugh Stand: Adventures in Humor, Peanut Butter and Jellyfishes: A Very Silly Alphabet Book, "Washing Adam's Jeans" and Other Painless Tricks for Memorizing Social Studies Facts, and two poetry books. Mr. Cleary lives in Cleveland, Ohio.

BRIAN GABLE is the illustrator of several Words Are CATegorical© books, as well as the Math Is CATegorical© series. Mr. Gable also works as a political cartoonist for the Globe and Mail newspaper in Toronto, Canada.

Text copyright © 2007 by Brian P. Cleary
Illustrations copyright © 2007 by Lerner Publishing Group, Inc.

All rights reserved. International copyright secured. No part of this book may be reproduced, stored in a retrieval system, or transmitted in any form or by any means—electronic, mechanical, photocopying, recording, or otherwise—without the prior written permission of Lerner Publishing Group, Inc., except for the inclusion of brief quotations in an acknowledged review.

Millbrook Press
A division of Lerner Publishing Group, Inc.
241 First Avenue North
Minneapolis, MN 55401 USA

For reading levels and more information, look up this title at www.lernerbooks.com.

Library of Congress Cataloging-in-Publication Data

Cleary, Brian P., 1959—
    Slide and slurp, scratch and burp : more about verbs / by Brian P. Cleary ;
illustrations by Brian Gable.
        p.   cm. — (Words are categorical)
    ISBN 978—0—8225—6207—8 (lib. bdg. : alk. paper)
    ISBN 978—0—8225—8805—4 (EB pdf)
    1. English language—Verb—Juvenile literature. I. Gable, Brian, 1949— ill.
II. Title. III. Series: Cleary, Brian P., 1959— Words are categorical.
PE1271.C57 2007
428.2—dc22   2006012096

Manufactured in China
9—41680—5250—3/23/2016